Time Management

Be Less Stressed By Completing Tasks In Less Time, And Achieve More Than You Ever Thought Possible

(Implementing Efficient Time Management To Generate Profits And Advance The Business)

Adrian Johnson

TABLE OF CONTENT

Introduction 1

Chapter 1: Time Management Secrets Only Successful Individuals Know 13

Setting Up Goals 18

Chapter 2: Create A Support Network Of Acquaintances And Family Members. 28

Chapter 3: Prioritizing Organizational Priorities Is Essential 31

Chapter 4: Day 7-Failure Is Assured If You Do Not Comply 40

Chapter 5: Worst Time Management Errors And Corrective Measures 45

Chapter 6: Tips For Mastering Workplace Time Management 61

Chapter 7: What Is Time Administration? 67

Chapter 8: Always Remember To Have Fun 84

Chapter 9: Morning Routines 100

Chapter 10: Avoiding Delays Number 107

Chapter 11: A Psychological Understanding Of Time Management 119

Chapter 12: Time Management For Enhanced Productivity 126

Chapter 13: Combine Tasks 138

Introduction

HOW DO WE MANAGE TIME?

Time management essentially entails prioritizing the completion of your most important duties. The less important but frequently time-consuming tasks should be delayed or, if possible, delegated.

The methods of time management are typically aimed at answering two questions: What are my most essential responsibilities? How do I allocate my limited working hours to these tasks?

There are numerous approaches and suggestions for answering these concerns. The following are the most essential (and frequently requested) time management techniques. The

Eisenhower Standard: Concentrate and Delegate Competently The so-called Eisenhower principle is a very well-known and popular instrument. It aids in prioritizing your own duties and identifying the most essential tasks. A coordinate system is used for this purpose, with one axis representing the importance and the other representing the urgency.

Many of us have been so conditioned to be constantly active that lounging around doing nothing may appear stressful.

We feel as though we are missing out on opportunities to advance our careers, create memories with our peers, and assist our loved ones. We feel guilty when we slumber when we should be working or doing something more productive.

It may take some time before you can fully appreciate the free time in your newly decluttered calendar, but it will be well worth the time and effort it takes to get there.

In a world filled with commotion and constant distractions, sitting in silence requires effort. That is not to say that all of your free time must be spent doing nothing, but meditating or praying regularly is beneficial for your mind, body, and spirit.

Are your mornings spent frantically attempting to get yourself and your children out the door? To make your mornings less chaotic, schedule additional discretionary time.

Get up somewhat early. Take care of some duties the night before to make the morning run more smoothly. The morning establishes the tone for the remainder of the day.

Having discretionary time on your calendar provides you with additional breathing room in the event that your obligations run longer than anticipated. It also allows you the flexibility to accept last-minute invitations.

When your schedule is full, you must reflexively decline new opportunities that arise. Choosing to be less busy encourages you to be more intentional with your time and align it with your highest priorities.

"Time is an artifact. To say 'I don't have time' is equivalent to saying 'I don't want to.

I cannot claim that every day goes exactly as planned. That is simply not possible. Nonetheless, I can affirm unequivocally that we now lead the lifestyle we desire. We focus our efforts on the things we hold most dear.

We still do not complete everything. Occasionally, we miss the mark. But we are headed in the correct direction. We have close, meaningful relationships with the people we love, and we are utilizing our skills and experiences to accomplish (what we perceive to be) purposeful activities.

Every person's existence is unique. What is significant to me may not be significant to you. The "plan of attack" to regain control of our schedules will be different.

Methods to Clear Your Agenda and Live Your Desired Life

Recognize the reality that you cannot accomplish everything.

We can only accomplish so much. We have limitless options but limited means. We must make crucial decisions to eliminate certain items. When we feel especially productive and superhuman, we find it difficult to accept this truth. But we cannot do everything. We must eliminate the debris.

Clutter is what prevents us from living the life we desire. It hinders our ability to accomplish the things we value most. It is a distraction that does not assist us in achieving our goals. Furthermore, it must be eradicated.

Clarify what is most essential...to you!

The things that are most essential to you will influence the decisions you make and how you spend your days. Why bother building a path if you have no idea where you're going? Prior to developing a strategy, you must establish your goals and the principles by which you will compete. Prior to determining how, you must determine what and why.

You'll require clarification in at least three crucial areas:

Which character of individual do you aspire to be?

Which relationships do you value the most?

What do you hope to achieve?

Determine what you must do to achieve these goals.

Once you have chosen your objective, you can begin to consider how you will achieve it. It is of the utmost importance to establish your goals and values. But if you don't take the second step and formulate a plan to achieve them, they remain aspirations.

You must map out a route to your objective. You must determine the most effective way to be and do what you desire. You must determine what actions and resources will be required to complete the task. If we don't, we run the risk of being enslaved by our circumstances and wandering aimlessly through existence.

Say "no" to additional items that hinder you.

It is not sufficient to know what actions you should take. You must also gain clarity regarding the types of actions you should avoid. Our time is limited, as has already been established. We will have to determine how we will devote our time. We must say "no" to some things in order to say "yes" to others.

Unavoidably, we will encounter circumstances that may derail us and make us want to abandon our goals. Sometimes these obstacles result from detrimental behaviors. Occasionally, they are created by those who wish for our failure. They are occasionally triggered by pleasant things that are not the finest.

Regardless of what causes the obstacles, we must pay attention to them and determine which activities must be eliminated!

Find your inspiration and apply it.

Examine yourself and determine what makes you special. What brings you to life? What humanizes you and reminds you that you are not just an automaton with a job and a bank account? What moves your emotions? What brings to mind the things you value most?

It could be listening to music, blogging, dancing, drawing, singing, running, or weightlifting, or anything else that you find utterly peculiar and unique.

It is acceptable if it is unrelated to your "greater purpose" and even if it makes logic to others. If it compels you and it's lawful, you should do it!

Life is too brief to live in perpetual discontentment.

Do not allow trivial matters to rob you of the life you could be savoring. Take an in-depth look at your existence and be sincere. Complete the task and clear your schedule. You can succeed!

Chapter 1: Time Management Secrets Only Successful Individuals Know

strategy for time management.It began as an initiative to increase manufacturing productivity by focusing on the efficiency of individual workers, quickly spread to the workplace, and ultimately encompassed the home environment as well.Taylor standardized work methods and tools in search of the best method for each endeavor in order to increase productivity.

Taylorism led to the modification of organizational structures.Prior to this, the majority of businesses and organizations were housed in private residences or small enterprises with open workspaces.There were no communication barriers, so employees could readily share their thoughts. Instead, offices and production areas were separated, work became more specialized, procedures were codified, and productivity increased. Unfortunately, communication was diminished. At least temporarily, productivity trumped interpersonal connections. Taylor did not intend for this to occur. He desired to make the employee's work easier while simultaneously increasing their productivity. This was his intention, although he did not coin the expression "work smarter, not harder."

Frank and Lillian Gilbreth also made a difference by incorporating time and motion research into the manufacturing process. The film Cheaper by the Dozen was inspired by the life of the Gilbreth family, which consisted of twelve children. They demonstrated that the same business principles that are used in the workplace can be applied at home. The result of their work is industrial engineering, time studies, incentive standards, and the constant pursuit of efficiency in offices and factories.

2

Why I Use My Time Efficiently

An Examination of Private Time Management Most of us think of personal time management when we consider time management. Personal time management can be loosely defined as managing our time so that we spend less time on things we must do and more time on things we desire.

Time management is frequently described as a set of skills; the assumption is that once we have mastered the skills, we will be happier, more organized, and more productive.

Whether or not you agree with this statement, enhancing any or all time management skills will unquestionably benefit any employee.

Five Reasons Your Business Should Learn Time Management

What Is the Most Valuable Good in the World?

Now, your response is inaccurate if it was materialistic. We are discussing time here. Have you ever pondered what distinguishes successful entrepreneurs from unsuccessful ones? Effective time management is the answer.

Setting Up Goals

These days, the term 'goals' is frequently used. So much, that it is frequently unclear what a very objective is.

Are resolutions and objectives comparable to objectives?

Why must we establish objectives?

According to research conducted by a scientist and career coach at Dominican University of California, there is an immediate correlation between setting goals and achieving success. Properly defined objectives facilitate the initiation of new behaviors and help you focus on what is essential for your success.

Each year, do you make comparable New Year's resolutions? Does one recommit to the same objective, promising to ultimately achieve it? If you answered yes, you should realize you are not alone.

Many people are caught in a cycle of setting goals, forgetting them or failing to complete them, and then setting similar goals again with a renewed (but temporary) resolve to achieve them.

You will be able to end the cycle, however. Continue reading to learn about the goal-setting process and maximize the performance of your organization, team, and yourself.

What are objectives, and what are they not?

Before establishing goals, it is necessary to understand what a goal is.

A objective is a list of desired accomplishments. It is the desired outcome that you or a group of people set out to achieve.

Goals are typically lengthy. They pertain to the life and career plans of individuals or the long-term objectives of a business or organization.

A objective is essentially a dream with a deadline.

Still a little perplexed? The characteristics of objectives and what they are not are listed below.

A target is:

Your perspective on the future. Goals should be the result of thorough consideration of a personal vision statement and desired outcomes.

Time-sensitive. Effective objectives are time-sensitive. Typically, goals have a lengthy time frame. They will then be broken down into shorter, more manageable objectives.

Large in nature. Don't be hesitant to line a seemingly unattainable objective. Feel free to think creatively and to dream large. You can set smaller, short-term objectives to help you reach your long-term objective.

A aim is not the same as: an objective. In contrast to goals, which describe what you desire to accomplish, objectives are the actions taken to achieve the goal. For instance, "I want to become an assured public speaker" could be an objective. By the end of this month, I will be able to develop my public speaking skills with the assistance of a teacher.

A resolution. Typically, resolutions are transient and provide instant gratification (as opposed to delayed gratification). A resolution is a call to do or refrain from doing something, whereas a goal is what you desire to accomplish.

A mission. Mission statements produce a clear and centered course of action. It is the purpose statement from which an organization, corporation, or individual operates. In contrast, a goal is a specific objective toward which you or your team labor.

Personal aims setting advice

Let's examine three guidelines for setting personal objectives.

1. Consider your passions

Part of the process for establishing life objectives should involve determining what inspires you and what your values are. You must be addicted to your goals if you desire to achieve them over the long term.

Your objectives should be meaningful and provide you with a sense of accomplishment when attained.

2. Set objectives {you can, you'll, you'll be able to} management

If your objective is contingent on an external factor, you will not be able to control whether or not you actually achieve it.

Your personal objectives should not be addictive to others. In addition, they should not be dependent on external factors over which you have no control.

Consider what you can and cannot take primary responsibility for.

3. Imagine your future

Consider what you'd like your existence to look like in detail. What does your optimal future look like?

For instance, if you are setting personal career objectives, you should ask yourself some questions that will point you in the correct direction.

How much money does one desire to earn? Do you wish to determine for yourself? What percentage of hours per day do you intend to complete?

Even if these questions do not explicitly help you choose a job, they will help you determine what your career goals should not be.

10 suggestions to achieve your objectives

Setting objectives is just the beginning. After identifying your objectives, attaining them may be an entirely different ballgame.

At times, pursuing your objectives can feel overpowering. Here are some effective goal-setting recommendations for achieving life objectives as easily as possible.

1. Have sensible objectives

Your objectives will not be attained if they are not SMART. If you haven't already noticed, SMART goals are goals that are: Specific. There is no point in setting vague objectives that do not accomplish anything specific. Investigation by the creators

In ninety percent of studies, philosopher & Latham discovered that specific and difficult goals lead to greater performance than basic goals, "do your best" goals, or no goals. It is essential that you and your team have well-defined objectives in order to avoid establishing goals that are too broad and, therefore, too challenging to achieve.

⯎ Measurable. Once a specific objective has been established, it is essential to be able to measure its success or achievement. This does not need to be in the traditional sense, such as on a numerical scale or a statistical scale; it should simply be measurable in some way, so that it is evident when you have reached or are about to reach your goal.

☐ Attainable. A reasonable objective must be within reach. Lean on data, analytics, and analysis to assist in setting attainable objectives.

☐ Relevant. Any goals established for organizations or individuals must align with company-wide objectives. Obviously, goal completion is necessary, and having goals met or worked towards is the overall objective when defining them; however, this is only beneficial if the goals are productive within the local environment and can contribute to the success of the organization. As a manager, it is crucial that you facilitate your employees' linking of their goals to team and company-wide objectives.

One of the most effective methods to inspire your staff is to ensure they understand how their contributions fit into the bigger picture.

Limited in time. Goals must be time-bound. It is ineffective to set a date too far in the future for a simple task or an unreasonably short deadline for something complex and time-consuming. This common pitfall is frequently demoralizing for employees. They are either left with an abundance of time during which they do not exert themselves, or they are left feeling stressed and unmotivated when they fail to complete objectives within the allotted time frame.

By establishing objectives with these characteristics, you position yourself for greater success.

Chapter 2: Create A Support Network Of Acquaintances And Family Members.

Single mothers can rely on a network of acquaintances and family members, as well as neighbors, for assistance when they need it. If someone offers you assistance, take it without hesitation.

Set some ground principles

Be clear with those you rely on for assistance with child care, grocery purchasing, homework, and the like. Set a reasonable and responsible amount that you anticipate requesting, so that your helper does not feel uncomfortable assisting you when your needs are unmet.

Avoid requesting rent, bills, or other financial assistance from companions. Accept financial assistance for child care or sustenance if offered. Even if they cannot pay, you should not take it personally. When you request assistance from a loved one, be gracious and say "thank you" if they offer to assist.

Set a positive example

If your needs are not being met because your spouse or companion is frequently absent, make it a priority to set a good example for your children. Spend significant time with them. Provide them with as much love and affection as you can. Let them know that you will be there for them while their father is abroad.

Be willing to aid.

The proverb "it takes a village to raise a child" applies to single parents. You're not alone. You simply need to know where to go when your demands are unmet. Do not squander valuable energy worrying about things outside of your control. Take charge and parent responsibly.

Look after yourself

No one else can assist your children emotionally and physically if you cannot. Parent while remaining healthful. The more time and effort you devote to self-care, the better parent you will be.

Chapter 3: Prioritizing Organizational Priorities Is Essential.

Determine and implement an effective organizing system. Use your phone's calendar or notes app to keep track of your tasks and appointments. Review your schedule weekly to determine if you will need to contact your support network at any point during the week.

Each week, I schedule a certain quantity of time away from the children. Approximately twelve hours per week. On most weekends, I spend the day after school drop-off at a friend's house, and then I collect up the children after school. I'll have the children from Thursday evening to Monday evening for a week-long weekend. Evenings are spent either playing a family game (such as charades or Battleship) or spending quality time together. If the weather permits, we will visit the park.

We are repeatedly told that mothers must be available 24/7. It's utter nonsense. We do not need to be constantly accessible. We must establish limits for what we can reasonably handle.

Consider your physical limitations with realism

Consider your body and how it reacts to your offspring with realism. There will be times when you will need a quick energy snack in order to keep up with your children and maintain a conversation with your peers. You will have no time to unwind after a long day. You will need to establish and adhere to your limits. You're not doing it correctly if you're constantly on the precipice of tears.

Practice saying no, and then don't be afraid to state it when necessary.

We have always said "yes" to our children's requests, regardless of whether we had the energy, time, or motivation to provide the expected level of attention and care. We're simply not good at setting limits, so we set "yes" as the default and become inundated by the results.

7) Delegate

Not in the mood to tackle a large project? Divide it into smaller duties and delegate them to other team members. As with most aspects of running a business, this is often overlooked by novice business owners, but it's a really excellent idea. Delegation not only enables you to focus on other projects or higher-level responsibilities as a leader or owner, but it also expedites the completion of work (when done correctly).

Remember: Your employees are not merely resources; if you invest in them and give them opportunities to flourish, they can become leaders in their own right. If you have multiple employees, you should not be afraid to designate tasks based on their respective strengths and weaknesses. Suppose, for instance, that one of your two-year-old employees excels at social media marketing, while another has experience creating websites. If you require a new website, delegate this responsibility to the second employee, as he or she will be superior in this area. The former employee may be better suited for writing compelling social media posts about your brand, and delegating these duties is likely to increase his or her level of engagement in other areas of his or her job description.

In other words, by assigning distinct duties to distinct individuals, you're letting everyone know what they're best at, which makes everyone happier. Recent research indicates that cheerful employees are more productive than unhappy employees. When allocating these tasks to your employees, don't forget to explain why certain tasks were selected over others.

Even though they may already know what they're greatest at and how well they do it because they work together every day, there may be times when someone else could perform a task more effectively (e.g., someone with experience working with customers over someone without such experience).

Explain why someone else should manage a specific task so that everyone understands their position within the organization and has enough respect for them to delegate responsibilities.

In addition to explaining why you've delegated particular tasks, be sure to establish deadlines and expectations. If no deadline is specified, when can they anticipate to receive it? What is expected of them once a mission has been completed? Ensure that your employees understand their duties within your organization so that there is no confusion regarding what must be done and by when. And bear in mind that unforeseen events can occur! If an employee informs you that he/she will not be able to complete a task by the deadline, inform the employee whether he/she must work overtime or request additional time from a teammate. Alternatively, you can propose to complete the task yourself. However, you should endeavor to be adaptable.

Your employees will respect you as long as you are transparent and establish clear expectations. Keep a record of every detail: From simple tasks, such as taking notes during meetings, to more complex tasks, such as pondering ideas for product development, jotting down key points, and keeping track of potential partnerships, organization is essential. When working on multiple projects simultaneously, it's easy to overlook important details, particularly if we're juggling several large projects. Keeping track of everything ensures that nothing falls through the cracks and significantly improves our prospects of success.

8) Avoid Multitasking

For the majority of individuals, multitasking appears to be a highly effective method to accomplish more in less time. Multitasking entails performing two tasks simultaneously, correct? Well, that depends on your definition of once. If you're using that time to do two separate activities (such as talking on your cell phone while driving), then yes, your brain is multitasking. However, if you're referring to doing multiple things simultaneously, then no, there is no scientific evidence that this actually increases productivity.

In fact, research indicates that people who attempt to juggle too many tasks tend to make more errors and take longer to complete their work than those who focus on a single task. Therefore, the next time you feel overwhelmed by your responsibilities, grant yourself permission to concentrate on a single task for as long as possible before shifting gears. Small improvements may not seem like much now, but over time they will add up and help you achieve success sooner rather than later. Here are some suggestions to help you accomplish this:

- Avoid postponing work: There are a million reasons why we don't want to do something, but only one reason why we should. Frequently, we use procrastination as an excuse to avoid difficult duties or situations that cause us anxiety or discomfort.

Problematically, whenever we delay taking action toward our goals, our motivation tends to erode further; thus, delaying something today could lead to delaying something tomorrow, which could lead to delaying something the following day, and so on, until nothing gets done. Remember that procrastination has never helped anyone accomplish anything noteworthy, despite how simple it may be to come up with excuses for why you shouldn't immediately begin working on something. And since every worthwhile objective requires a degree of discomfort, it is best to confront these concerns head-on rather than waiting for them to disappear on their own.

In other words, fear does not imply error; therefore, cease making excuses and start getting things done! Most successful individuals.

- Limit distractions: When attempting to focus on a large undertaking, distractions can be extremely alluring. After all, new emails, social media updates, text messages, and phone calls are entertaining and exciting, especially when they provide opportunities for engaging conversations with trusted friends or the delivery of fascinating news stories. However, if you allow yourself to become distracted every time something intriguing occurs during the workday, you will likely accomplish nothing. Set aside specific periods each day to check your inboxes and respond to urgent messages so that they don't distract you from other tasks.

Chapter 4: Day 7-Failure Is Assured If You Do Not Comply

" Each person is required to remove one day. A day in which one deliberately separates the past from the future. Occupations, family, supervisors, and companions can exist without us one day, and if our self-images permit us to acknowledge it, they could continue to exist in perpetuity in our absence. Every person deserves a day off in which no problems are confronted and no arrangements are sought. Each of us must withdraw from considerations that will not withdraw from us."

— Maya Angelou

Congratulations! You now understand everything you need to know to become an expert of your time and efficacy and a member of the top 1%.

Once you've put in a full week utilizing all the techniques in this book, you'll be far ahead of your peers and wondering how you ever managed to complete work without these techniques.

That will occur in one week; today, we recuperate.

Yes, the massive R word. I realize that it can be incredibly challenging for high-caliber employees like you to imagine a day without any business-related activity. I labored too. The possibility of not checking email, writing the next section, organizing the upcoming week, or evaluating my goals was practically intolerable. Every last piece of it seemed more important than requesting a day off.

I was extremely off-target. Remember that you earned this.

You require this.

You will benefit from this action.

Permit me to reiterate the obvious: you are not an automaton. To maintain your optimal level of performance, you must revitalize. Taking some time off is in no way a sign of weakness; rather, it is a sign of respect for your body. If you do not take one full day off per week, regardless of the techniques you employ, you will gradually become less and less productive. It is known as burnout, and it eventually affects everyone who does not get sufficient leisure when required.

It might appear unusual; you'd think the easiest way to reach your goals would be to go full speed ahead, 24 hours per day. However, numerous studies indicate that individuals are more productive after returning from an entire day off than if they had never taken one.

Therefore, what constitutes a complete day off? Typically, this depends on the individual. Each person develops in an unexpected manner. The goal is to feel less anxious, less agitated, and completely at ease by the end of the day. For example, on my three day weekend yesterday, I: - Woke up at 11am - Went for a long walk - Had a pleasant breakfast with my family - Attended a Japanese Culture Festival - Drank a messy gin martini while watching the sunset - Ate Thai food with a friend I hadn't seen in a while - Went to a bar with friends - Watched a movie

- Slept

It was a completely relaxing day, and I awoke the next morning feeling refreshed and ready to take on the world.

Maintain as a top priority: this was my method of relaxation.

Yours could be as simple as going to the beach, spending time with the family, or writing; it makes no difference. Nobody can dictate how you should unwind.

Chapter 5: Worst Time Management Errors And Corrective Measures

Time management is currently all the rage, and it's simple to see why. The majority of individuals, especially small business proprietors and entrepreneurs, work themselves to the bone.

It has been determined that 70% of us work outside of office hours and on weekends. The numbers represent an annual average of 240 hours of unpaid overtime per worker across all employment types. Based on a standard 38-hour work week, this equates to over six weeks of unpaid labor per worker per year.

We work from our beds, while enjoying dinner, and on vacation. This negatively impacts our relationships, health, and efficiency.

It is not surprising that we seek as much time management advice as we can. Unfortunately, a significant portion of this information is so useless that it sets you up for failure.

There are numerous factors that lead to poor time management, so here are 12 of the most common errors made by solo entrepreneurs and small business owners, along with solutions to help you manage your time more effectively.

You believe there is insufficient time.

We've all been culpable of believing that time is limited. When we examine our to-do lists and calendar, we feel overburdened. If I had more time today, I could accomplish everything.

Everyone has the same 24 hours per day. Some individuals can make the most of this limited amount of time because they have acknowledged the problem and taken action.

The solution is that complaining about not having enough time will not magically grant you more time. It may provide temporary relief, but only temporarily. It does not address the fundamental cause, which may be your poor time management.

To initiate change, you must acknowledge that there is sufficient time; you simply do not know how to make the most of it. You can now begin to improve your time management.

2. Believing that a single solution suits all situations

You have acknowledged that there is a problem and are searching the internet for solutions. You should feel pleased about taking this initial step. You will quickly realize that there is no one-size-fits-all solution after perusing just two or three posts.

Rather than relying on a tool with all the bells and flourishes, determine where you're struggling and what's most important to you.

For instance, if scheduling is distracting you from product development, you could use a scheduling tool like Calendar that automates the majority of your scheduling requirements through machine learning. Consider utilizing a tool like SaneBox to manage your inbox if you're spending too much time on email.

This may not be the most exciting advice, but by identifying your problem areas and priorities, you can find the optimal solution for your needs.

Not differentiating between being occupied and productive

We fall victim to this time management fallacy when we believe that being occupied equates to being productive. It's wonderful that you spent the last few hours clearing out your inbox and interacting with customers on social media. However, was that the most productive use of your time at the time?

I honestly believe that many people grapple with the concept of "busy versus productive."

Here is how you can be productive as opposed to just busy:

Identify what is both essential and essential, as opposed to focusing on what can wait.

Implement a strategic organizational plan. For instance, I have a nightly routine in which I lay out my clothes, list my three most essential tasks, review my schedule, and ensure I have all of my equipment for the following day. A little preparation the night before guarantees a productive day.

Eliminate distractions, like email and text messages.

Don't stress about being flawless.

Say 'yes' only to time requests that serve a purpose.

Be willing to make certain sacrifices, such as leaving a no longer beneficial organization.

Surround yourself with productive individuals.

Weigh the pros and cons of a trend before adopting it.

Be honest about your progress.

4. Believing that following a particular system will reduce anxiety

It is true that effective time management can reduce anxiety. Depending on the time management system you choose, however, you should ensure that it does not contribute to your stress.

Consider the popular Getting Things Done method. This system requires five steps: capturing, clarifying, organizing, reflecting, and acting on all of your obligations. This includes phone messages, email correspondence, meetings, shopping, and housework. This will cause anxiety and overwhelm for some.

Time management is only useful if you are aware of your limitations and don't let the system dictate your entire life and contribute to your anxiety over finding time. In other words, if you don't proceed with caution (especially initially), time management can increase your tension levels.

Recognizing this is the first step in locating a time management system that meets your specific requirements.

5. erroneously estimating the time required for specific duties

Suppose you wish to compose a blog post for your website. You schedule an hour for this activity. You end up spending two hours, and your entire schedule is abruptly thrown off.

Indeed, setting a deadline for certain tasks can motivate you to complete them within the allotted time frame. Occasionally, this is impossible, and you have underestimated the time required to complete this task.

The most effective solution is to monitor your time for a couple of weeks. You can do this manually by recording your daily activities in a notebook and calculating how long each will take to determine if your expectations are realistic.

Additionally, you can use time-tracking software such as Toggl or RescueTime. By having a more precise understanding of how you spend your days, you can allocate the appropriate amount of time to specific activities.

concentrating on time management rather than assignment management

Time management is less effective than task management because tasks have defined boundaries, making them simpler to manage. You are aware of when you began working on a project and when it was completed. One restricted article at a time is permitted.

"Task management is the process of managing a task through its different stages: planning, development, and completion," Laura Sima writes in the Teamweek Journal. "It functions both individually and collectively by motivating individuals to achieve their goals.

The concept of time is not precisely defined; therefore, a task management system could help you be more precise with your time management.

Sima explains, "Effective task management includes all the steps from planning to assigning a priority, including status, outlining the required resources for completion, notifications, and observation." "Tools such as online calendars, workflow software, and project management software will assist you in outlining various projects, tasks, and their respective statuses."

Always seize low-hanging produce.

You have just settled in for the day at work and are eager to begin completing your tasks. Which tasks are you going to prioritize first thing in the morning? You will most likely choose the simplest, least time-consuming task or an essential item. If you are able to cross ten items off your list, you will consider the day a success.

Remember the entire concept of being occupied and productive? Even if you accomplish a lot, it does not necessarily mean that your time was well-spent or focused on the areas where you would make the most progress.

Solution: If you want to use your time more efficiently, avoid picking the low-hanging fruit, or the easiest duties. Focus your efforts on your highest priorities, and be aware of which tasks will yield the most output. Find a means to automate, delegate, or save mundane tasks for times when your energy is low.

8. believing that rising earlier will afford you more time

Many people suggest that if you want to enhance your time management, you must rise early. I've found that waking up early is the most productive time of day for me. However, this does not work for everyone, particularly night enthusiasts.

If you wake up early, you cannot remain awake all night. You must establish a bedtime regimen and adhere to it.

If you are not a morning person, do not attempt to alter. No one can function effectively with a brain that is overtired. Instead, your schedule should be based on your circadian rhythm. Simply stated, the most productive time to work is when you are most attentive and alert.

9. Believing you can decrease your burden

It is easy to believe that if you organize your days effectively, you will have a lighter workload. Unfortunately, this is not true. According to Parkinson's Law, if we have an open slot in our schedule, we will occupy it.

You may have completed the day's most essential tasks, but it's highly likely that you'll add even more items to your calendar or to-do list so that there are no blank spaces.

Remember, when it comes to productivity, to adhere to the 80/20 rule, which states that 20 percent of your efforts produce 80 percent of your results. Use the time to meditate, ponder, or add flexibility to your schedule, as opposed to piling on even more work.

Chapter 6: Tips For Mastering Workplace Time Management

Take care of the first item on your list so that you do not waste time and energy moving on to the next. Time can be set aside for responding to emails, phone messages, etc. To be a distraction, you must immediately respond to all incoming emails and text messages. Turn off your phone and email alerts to avoid having to examine them at inappropriate times.

resisted the urge to combine

This is one of the most fundamental time management techniques, but also one of the most difficult to implement. Turn off all devices and concentrate solely on the task at hand. Multitasking is enticing, but it will only cause you to shoot yourself in the foot. Changing between tasks is inefficient and reduces productivity. Similarly, a mile-long list of tasks should not overwhelm you. Take steady inhalations and exhalations and focus on one task at a time; worrying about it will not make it go faster.

Assign tasks time limits

Rather than working until a task is complete, you should set time limits for it as part of your planning approach. To-do lists are beneficial, but they may give you the impression that you are never completing anything.

The Pomodoro Technique can help you complete your to-do list in 25-minute intervals with brief breaks in between and a longer break after four if you wish to maintain a consistent level of productivity. This method combines focused concentration with periodic breaks to prevent mental fatigue and maintain motivation.

Include delays

Include breaks in your daily regimen. Rest your body after completing a task. What you do to recharge your batteries is irrelevant. You can go for a stroll or play ping-pong.

Master the craft of refusal

You will never learn how to manage your time at work if you cannot say no. You are the only person who knows how much time you have, so do not be afraid to decline a request that would prevent you from completing more important tasks. Also, do not be afraid to abandon an endeavor that is failing.

Instead of performing numerous low-value duties, perform a few high-value jobs. Keep in mind the 80/20 rule: 20% of your inputs account for 80% of your output. Focus your energies in that direction.

Delegate it if you can't say no. Delegation may be a difficult skill to master, but it can help you better manage your time. Determine which responsibilities you can delegate now that a talented team has been assembled.

Organize yourself

This suggestion should be added to your to-do list for time management purposes. If you have numerous documents scattered across your desk, it will be difficult to locate the one you require. Few things are more frustrating than squandering time searching for lost items, not to mention how difficult it is to concentrate when surrounded by a great deal of clutter.

It's the small things that matter. Create a system for categorizing documents. Unsubscribe from any email lists you no longer wish to receive. Consider the fact that you only need to do it once, but the benefits will last a lifetime.

Eliminate every source of distraction

Due to social media, online browsing, coworkers, text messages, and instant messaging, the number of workplace distractions may be infinite. Personal time management requires proactive elimination of these obstacles. Close your door to avoid interruptions. Close all windows except the one you are currently working on. Put your phone calls on pause until after lunch, and disable text message notifications.

Begin by taking baby measures. Identify your top two distractions and make a two-week commitment to eliminating them. Remember that getting enough sleep, drinking plenty of water, and eating a nutritious diet can help you maintain focus at work, especially when the afternoon slump comes.

Chapter 7: What Is Time Administration?

What Does Time Management Entail?

Time management is the process of organizing available time and regulating the quantity of time spent on specific activities in order to function more efficiently.

Some individuals have an easier time managing their time than others, but everyone can develop routines to improve their time management skills. Without effective time management, your work and health may suffer, and you may produce subpar work.

Missing deadlines

Increasing your level of tension

destroying your work-life equilibrium

damaging your professional standing

Why is time management so crucial?

Time management is essential because it enables you to schedule your workday so that you can grow your business without sacrificing your work-life balance. Here are some benefits of effective time management:

Enhance Your Efficiency

You'll have a clearer idea of what you need to accomplish and how long each task should take once you've mastered the skill of allocating time for each of your essential responsibilities. When you have a schedule to adhere to, you will likely find that you spend less time deciding what to work on or procrastinating and more time performing essential tasks. Time management can help you focus on only the most important tasks and avoid time-consuming diversions.

Improve Your Work

When you're not constantly racing to meet a deadline, you can devote more time and consideration to your work. Time management allows you to prioritize your responsibilities and ensure you have sufficient time to complete each one. The quality of your work improves when you don't rush to complete it before a rapidly approaching deadline.

Complete Work on Time

To effectively organize your time, you must assign each item on your list to specific segments of time. Numerous individuals use time management to give themselves several days to complete a task, or to complete it in advance of the deadline to provide a buffer for potential problems. If you meticulously plan the time required to complete your assignment, you will always meet your deadlines.

Reduce Your Anxiety

It is simple to become anxious when you have a long list of personal and professional responsibilities. Good time management may enable you to prioritize your to-do list and allot the necessary time for your most important tasks, so that you are aware of precisely what you must complete and how much time you have available to do so. Prioritizing your responsibilities and allowing yourself sufficient time to complete them will help reduce your tension.

Enhanced Employment Opportunities

Time management may help you become a more reliable employee who always meets deadlines with high-quality work.

In turn, this can make you a more valuable employee and enhance your professional reputation, which can help you discover new opportunities to advance your career.

Boost Your Confidence

When you effectively manage your time and meet your deadlines, you will experience a sense of accomplishment and confidence in your abilities. Consistently completing your daily to-do list is a powerful motivator that can encourage individuals to enhance their time management skills and pursue new career opportunities.

Become More Efficient

When you learn how to effectively manage your time, you will become more focused at work, allowing you to accomplish more with less time.

For instance, instead of endeavoring to work on a large project in the fifteen minutes before a meeting, you can perform a few minor tasks and save the larger tasks that require more mental capacity for when you have a large block of free time. You will be able to work more efficiently and complete more tasks in less time.

Fundamentals of Time Management

Improving your time management abilities may increase your productivity and decrease your anxiety. Here are some fundamental time management techniques:

Plan Forward

Planning your time in advance is the most important factor in effective time management. Determine when you are most productive: perhaps you are most alert in the morning, or perhaps you hit your stride at night.

Save your most important and difficult tasks for times when your productivity is at its peak. Schedule simpler or less demanding tasks for times when you are less alert. Before beginning each day, you should have a firm understanding of how much time you will spend on each task on your to-do list.

Prioritize Tasks

Evaluate each task you must complete to determine which are the most important and essential, and make them your top priority for the day. Leave less important tasks or projects that have not yet become imperative for a time when you have more time to focus on them.

Eliminate Distraction

Distractions are one of the greatest hinderers of productivity. Social networking sites, mobile phones, and disruptive coworkers are all potential sources of distraction and schedule derailment. A third of employees are distracted for up to three hours per day. If you find that certain distractions are too tempting, try locking your smartphone in a desk compartment during the day or installing a browser extension that blocks your most distracting websites.

Don't Multitask

Multitasking may appear to be a terrific way to complete additional work, but it actually decreases your productivity. Instead of completing multiple tasks, you commence but do not complete any of them. For optimal time management, you should focus on a single task at a time and give it your full concentration while you're working to avoid making mistakes.

Reward Yourself for Excellence

Rewards can be an excellent motivator for time management. Give yourself a small reward for each task you complete throughout the day. For example, you could commemorate the completion of a report by taking a 15-minute walk outside. Rewards can help you attain a better work-life balance by keeping you engaged at work.

What is objective setting?

Some individuals may have difficulty adhering to their goals because they do not distinguish between their goals and their daily self-improvement efforts. The decision to begin jogging every day does not always constitute a deliberate objective. Therefore, let's examine what objective setting entails.

The first step in goal-setting is to establish a new objective, skill, or endeavor that you desire to achieve. Then, you devise a plan for achieving the objective and work to achieve it.

Instead of merely jogging for no particular purpose, a meaningful objective would be to begin a training program for a specific event, such as a half marathon on Thanksgiving Day, which requires much more meticulous planning, motivation, and discipline.

Why is establishing goals so important?

When you set goals, you take charge of the trajectory of your life or your career. Objectives foster concentration. The decisions you make and the actions you take should bring you closer to your goals.

Setting goals keeps you motivated, increases your enjoyment, and significantly benefits your business. When you set goals, you create a vision of what your life or business could look like. Then you challenge yourself and your team to achieve the best results possible.

How to establish goals

If goals are so important, why do we fail to achieve them? Because we do not plan the necessary actions.

A goal planning method requires you to consider the journey (i.e., how you will carry out your responsibilities) as well as the destination. Review the procedures listed below to get started.

Consider the outcomes you wish to achieve.

Before deciding on a specific objective, you should examine your objectives in greater detail and ask yourself the following questions:

Is this an objective you seek?

Is it important enough to warrant hours of time and effort?

If you are unwilling to invest time, it may not be worthwhile to pursue.

If you create an extensive list of goals to pursue simultaneously, it may be difficult to achieve any of them. Instead, use the queries above to determine which handfuls of goals are the most important right now, and then focus on those handfuls.

Establish SMART objectives

Once you have honed in on what you truly desire, verify that your objective meets the SMART criteria:

- Specific

- Measurable

- Attainable

- Realistic

- Time-limited

The most important aspect of SMART goal setting is making your objective explicit so that you can readily measure your progress and determine if you've achieved it. The greater the specificity of your objective, the greater the likelihood that you will achieve it.

For instance, many people set goals to lose weight, but they don't always specify how much weight they want to lose or when they want to accomplish this goal. A specific objective could be "I want to lose 25 pounds before the end of the year." This objective specifies a precise weight reduction target and completion date.

Document your objectives

When you write down your goals, they become concrete and tangible, as opposed to vague concepts that exist only in your imagination. Once you've written down your objectives, maintain them in a visible location, such as on your mirror or near your computer screen for personal goals, on the walls next to everyone's workstations for team goals, and in internal presentations for business objectives.

This strategy encourages daily progress toward your objectives. Employ a positive tone when writing down your goals so that you remain motivated to achieve them.

Create a plan of action

Many individuals establish a goal, but never develop a detailed action plan outlining how they will achieve it. Your action plan should include both the overarching goal you're aiming to achieve and a list of the necessary steps to get there.

Don't be afraid to be creative with your plan of action. Recall your elementary school days and be creative. Using crayons, markers, or colored pencils, record your goal.

Create a timeline

Utilize a timeline builder as part of your action plan to help visualize the responsibilities, activities, milestones, and deadlines necessary to achieve your objective. After establishing these dates, make every effort to adhere to them precisely. A deadline creates a sense of urgency, which in turn motivates you to stay on track and accomplish your goal.

Take steps

Now that everything has been planned, it is time to take action. You did not exert so much effort only to neglect your objective. Each action you take should lead to the next until you reach your goal.

Re-evaluate and appraise your progress

You must maintain a high level of motivation to achieve your goal. Consider coordinating a weekly evaluation, which could include evaluating your progress and confirming your schedule.

Once you realize how close you are to the conclusion, you will be more motivated to see it through. If you're slightly behind schedule, make the necessary adjustments and continue.

Commence setting objectives

The practice of defining objectives expedites and improves achievement. It may fuel your desire and assist you in achieving tangible results. A goal planning approach can help you determine how to develop specific, expeditious, and reasonable objectives.

Chapter 8: Always Remember To Have Fun

The most essential thing to remember when running a home-based business is to always have fun, both at work and outside of it. You should always take the initiative wherever you go. Do something every day for your home-based business, even if it's not explicitly related.

Keeping your goals in mind will motivate and direct you to accomplish more. Be cautious not to become overly preoccupied with meticulous preparation, unless doing so is optimal for you. To work proactively despite any potential changes or impediments, you must examine your inner self. As long as you remember to have fun, everything will turn out well in the end.

ACTION STEPS FOR MORE PLEASURE
Making work pleasurable is one of the best ways to increase productivity in a

home-based business. You can take the following steps to achieve your goal of experiencing greater job satisfaction:

Create an inventory of tasks without including times. This affords you greater flexibility.

Estimate how long it will take to complete each of your duties, then leave enough time between tasks to take a break. If you are waiting for something, such as a stack of reports to be copied or coffee to brew, perform a mind-relaxing game or engage in an entertaining hobby.

Games that can be played over a period of time, such as chess or online card games, are an excellent way to pass the time while working.

• Keep a stress-relieving item on hand, such as a puzzle, that you can use whenever you feel overwhelmed. Puzzles and games that require thought and mental effort are the finest.

Plan extra time at the end of the day for leisure or to complete work that was not completed on time or arose unexpectedly.

Discuss non-work-related matters with your coworkers. If you are the only employee in your office and you are an entrepreneur, join a discussion room about a topic that interests you, such as working from home.

FUN ADDITIONAL SUGGESTIONS

Keeping an open mind when deciding what to do with your leisure time can be extremely beneficial for both you and your company. Learn a new skill, such as yoga, meditation, or even a conjuring trick, during this time. When things at work become stressful, taking a pause to engage in these types of activities is an excellent way to relax and unwind. Participate in group activities whenever possible.

Some individuals choose to utilize this leisure to get much-needed rest. Find a place where you won't be disturbed if you need peace and silence.

ADVANCED PRECAUTIONS

Whenever you are enjoying yourself at work, exercise common sense. For example, if you intend to take naps during your leisure time, you should keep an alarm clock on hand to avoid dozing off while you should be working.

Do not worry excessively about having fun until all necessary work has been completed, particularly if you have critical projects or deadlines to meet. Then, when things have settled down and you are no longer required to be as hands-on, you may consider taking more time off work.

Not all occupations provide enjoyable activities, so operating a home-based business is an added advantage.

Consider the Eisenhower Matrix at Work.
Julie organized her views using the time-management skills matrix as follows:
She was unable to check her email in the early morning because the stand-up session revealed QA divisional issues. She categorized the messages rather than marking them as something to discuss later because discussing a strategy was more crucial.

The customer who was scheduled to meet with Julie at noon arrived half an hour late to ask specific questions. She was aware that her son's field trip was still several weeks away, so she did not require information immediately. She could possibly discuss it with the instructor later that day. She rescheduled the appointment for 11:30 a.m. and the phone call for later so as not to keep her client waiting.

It became apparent around 4:00 p.m. that certain aspects of the undertaking required immediate attention. In contrast, Julie's son had fallen ill again the week prior and required medical attention. She delegated the responsibility of organizing the conference to her most reliable colleague because her son's health took precedence.

Consider the Eisenhower Matrix at Home.

Despite having an appointment, Tom and Julie had to wait longer for their test because the doctor's office was full. Julie asked her husband to do the grocery purchasing in case they were unable to complete it on time; Julie wanted to improve her overall fitness, so she worked out three times per week. However, as she was departing the office, a coworker called to remind her of their previous conversation. Some of their decisions required authorization. Julie rescheduled her workout so she could participate in a video conference with a few of the late-night workers. Today, assisting them in finishing so they could return home was more important and imperative than her exercise.

By 9:30 p.m., Julie was exhausted from visitors, conferences, the health clinic, and her children's activities. She desired nothing more than a restful night's slumber. She decided not to watch the movie because she knew that sleeping would benefit her far more than viewing television at that time.

As illustrated by Julie's diagram, the purpose of the time matrix is to teach us all how to make better decisions regarding our schedules. She did not need to overthink the tasks or the consequences of her actions because she knew precisely what she was doing. She was able to effectuate necessary alterations in a seamless and stress-free manner.

What Sets the Time Matrix Apart from Other Methods?

This strategy has nothing to do with acquiring new skills and everything to do with enhancing your reasoning. It will assist you in gaining a clearer understanding of your goals and how you spent your time or contributed to your current position. Thus, you will be better able to coordinate and plan for the future.

It will result in a positive change after some time has elapsed. You will observe how much easier it is to plan your work and how much more adept you have become at handling minor setbacks and impending constraints.

Attempting to manage time is becoming obsolete in some respects. Coaches and efficiency experts recommend that you have the ability to manage your objectives and resources. We cannot create time because we lack it. Simply stated, we can utilize it more effectively. Instead of cramming as much as possible into a day, prioritize the essentials.

5.2 Warren Buffett's "2 List" Strategy

It can be exciting and motivating to write down your life objectives. It provides us with direction, clarifies our objectives, makes us all feel active, and gives the impression that we are advancing.

Have you ever created an inventory of your goals only to find that it was lengthy? Then, once action is taken, they are either forgotten or only partially accomplished? We are taught from a tender age to set goals; however, do all of these objectives limit us?

Buffet, one of the world's finest businessmen, questions the necessity of these goals. Rather, he attributes his success to eliminating irrelevant goals in order to focus on those that will lead to the desired outcomes.

With a net worth of more than seventy billion dollars and ownership of more than seventy businesses through his private equity firm Berkshire Hathaway, Warren Buffett has demonstrated that he knows a thing or two about prioritizing essential work.

This level of concentration does not, however, occur frequently. When there are numerous options available, the majority of us experience choice anxiety. Buffett has a solution, however.

According to a story told by Buffett's private pilot, Mike Flint, Buffett has a straightforward method for determining which work merits his attention. While Flint inquired as to which professional objectives should be prioritized, this strategy was implemented for both short- and long-term objectives.

When Flint and Buffett were discussing this endeavor, he consented to prioritize the five objectives Buffett had highlighted. However, because the remaining 20 were still important to him, he stated that he would work on them whenever he had the chance.

That is comprehensible. They were not terrible choices, but they were not among the top five. What was Buffett's refutation?

"No, Mike, you have it inverted. The items you did not circle comprised your list of items to avoid. You will not give attention to this information until you have completed your top five."

Why Do We Want to Eliminate 'Excellent' Lifestyle Options?

Buffett understood that even though there are "excellent" options or goals to pursue, everything on our previous list is solely a distraction in our daily lives.

It would be comparable to carrying your winter coat, shoes, and socks on a weekend trip to a sunny location. While being prepared is an admirable trait, you are carrying unnecessary baggage that is only slowing you down.

Every action and choice we make has associated expenses. And attempting to choose between focusing on your primary or secondary list diminishes your motivation and zeal.

On the other hand, wanting to get rid of unnecessary items and options is quite uncomplicated. It is difficult to let go of familiar objects. It is difficult to avoid squandering a substantial amount of time on activities that are simple to justify but provide little return. The activities that are most likely to impede your development are those that you consider essential but are not actually crucial.

Every action has repercussions. Even actions that appear neutral are not entirely impartial. They necessitate time, effort, and territory that could be better allocated to more essential responsibilities or better conduct. We are often in a state of motion as opposed to taking action.

This explains why Warren Buffett's strategy is so brilliant. Prioritize the first six items on your list until you reach the twenty-fifth. They are important to you. It is straightforward to justify giving them your focus. These items are a distraction compared to your top five goals. You had 20 incomplete assignments instead of five completed ones because you spent time on trivial matters.

Everything must be eradicated with a vengeance. Make a concentrated effort to focus. Complete a mission or else it will be eliminated.

The most apparent distractions, such as television and social media, are straightforward to identify and eliminate (or reduce). It is difficult to get rid of items that are important to you if you are unaware that they are distractions. These items may be labeled "secondary priority items."

Essentially, a bucket contains a list of aspirations and objectives that you hope to achieve in the future. Still, an unattainable list is a compilation of objectives that are actively pursued daily. The preposterous list compels you to take action immediately, as opposed to procrastinating until your funeral.

After achieving five main objectives, we will be different individuals. Your objectives and interests are likely to vary. Your business would occupy a distinct location. Your relatives will be in a different location. Restart with a new roster of 25 objectives.

It is essential to avoid the remaining 20 objects until you have mastered the first five. They can be alluring methods to waste your time and effort. The most productive individuals focus their efforts on a limited number of goals. Concentration and compartmentalization are essential for success.

Warren Buffett has demonstrated the value of his advice. Create a detailed inventory of your objectives and adhere to it. Create a list of your top 25 priorities and rank them immediately. Then concentrate on achieving your best five objectives!

5.3 The Ivy Lee Procedure

The Ivy Lee Technique has existed for nearly one hundred years. It is remarkably simple, yet remains highly relevant and effective due to its emphasis on prioritization and eliminating the unnecessary and trivial from your daily calendar.

Contrary to multitasking, which divides your attention across multiple projects, leaving you feeling occupied but never completing anything of substance, concentrating on a limited number of essential tasks throughout the day maximizes efficiency and productivity.

Give yourself no more than six essential tasks per day, rank them from most to least important, and then prioritize and complete them in that order. Do not move on to the next assignment until the previous one has been completed.

Create a list of your objectives for the following day at the conclusion of each workday. Repeat daily, transferring any unfinished tasks to the top of tomorrow's six-item list.

To maximize each day, it is necessary to optimize your calendar. This is especially true for new mothers: every minute saved at work is a minute spent with loved ones at home.

John Rampton, an entrepreneur, realized that his inefficient work habits were detrimental to his family because he frequently arrived home late and fatigued when his wife and infant daughter needed him most. A century-old "efficiency hack" enabled him to spend less time at work and more time at home relaxing.

According to the Ivy Lee technique, you must concentrate on one task at a time, working your way down the list from the most important to the least important until you have completed everything. Any unfinished tasks must be added to the six-task inventory for the following day.

By planning your day the night before, you can avoid mental fatigue and conserve energy for the most essential tasks. Instead of squandering valuable time and effort in the morning making decisions, you begin waking up knowing precisely what you'll be doing all day."

The Ivy Lee technique dates back to 1918, when Charles Schwab, the chairman of Bethlehem Steel Company, hired Lee, a production consultant, to help him increase the business's efficiency. According to legend, Lee gave Schwab his technique for free, and three months later, Schwab's chief was so impressed with the results that he sent Lee a check for $25,000 (approximately $400,000 today).

Additionally, the Ivy Lee method "eliminates the friction of beginning" a new task. By choosing your most important tasks the night before, you can avoid hesitation and time squander the following morning, allowing you to be more productive when it's time to begin.

Everything you did not accomplish today should be added to tomorrow's to-do list. If a task occupies too much of your time for multiple days in a row, consider whether it should have been on your to-do list. Something which takes numerous days or weeks to complete is typically not significant enough, to begin with. Restart from phase one the following day.

Chapter 9: Morning Routines

There is nothing simpler than doing nothing. When you stand up and become intentional about something, things become somewhat difficult and challenging to accomplish. As you alter your habits and become aware of your every action and thought, your mind will attempt to return you to your default setting so that things can return to "normal." Essentially, you must realize that your conscious mind may currently be aware of the desired change, and that all of this will make sense to it. The difficulty arises, however, when the subconscious must agree with the conscious consciousness.

You may believe that it is sufficient for your conscious mind to desire change, but you must realize that your subconscious mind always goes beyond acquiring new skills. This portion of your mind is responsible for the processing of information and your cognitive processes. It is responsible for preserving all information related to beliefs and values, as well as determining your memories and the information you observe in your environment. Your subconscious mind is responsible for informing your conscious mind of what to do, remember, and store for later. If there's anything you should be working to fix at this point, it's your subconscious, and as I've mentioned previously, it takes more than a few simple steps to get these changes inked as rapidly.

Discipline will play a significant role in unlearning old behaviors and adopting new ones. By practicing discipline, you will commit to mastering your time usage in a way that will alter your subconscious and turn this into a habit. Your subconscious will attempt to convince your conscious mind that you are operating abnormally when you make this change. Once you reach this point, you'll be overcome with the sensation that you shouldn't be doing what you're doing. Even though the conscious mind is aware that this is not in your best interest, the body is simply attempting to return you to a 'normal' state of functioning.

You will need to exert effort to adhere to the process, as working against your subconscious will not be easy. Therefore, having cheat days or engaging in activities that may cause you to disregard the process will not be beneficial. Instead, it will simply return you to your initial state of consciousness, which is undesirable.

A Morning Routine in Order for Discipline to Become Routine.

In reality, morning regimens are frequently portrayed as optional pastimes that can be performed whenever you have the time. While many may encourage it on the basis of self-care and learning to put yourself first, it is not emphasized enough in terms of its contribution to discipline.

When you have a structured morning routine, you learn to be disciplined and accountable for matters pertaining to your improvement. It begins with the little things, such as establishing a routine for waking up at a specific time each morning, in order to develop the habit of caring for your mental health and well-being.

The way we conduct our lives demonstrates that many of us believe that discipline is most important when there is a clear motivation to do something because someone else is involved. However, it should matter most when you are alone with yourself. You may presume that you are disciplined because you are always awake by 5 a.m. Monday through Friday. However, when you do not have to go to work or school, what time do you wake up? What time do you rise if your meeting or lecture begins at 11 a.m instead of 8 a.m? What then do you do?

Before you are coerced into doing something out of dread of a late warning or missed class, discipline must be your highest priority. You are the most important person, so discipline must begin with you. On days when you have the option to sleep in and would rather lounge in bed for a while, get up and begin your morning regimen so that you can be present for yourself. You can surely do the same for yourself if you can commit to showing up for others even when you feel least capable or willing.

When you have a structured morning routine, you will be able to begin the day in a positive manner, which will contribute to a good, successful, and fruitful day. Nurturing your mind, body, and soul by beginning your day with affirmations and habits that will flow into you so that you can remain devoted and committed to things that will benefit you will prepare you to face the day in a positive and focused manner.

Your morning routine does not have to be identical to that of others. The purpose of a morning routine is to discover personalized ways to infuse the best into oneself. A healthy breakfast every morning may provide me with comfort and contentment. However, those who do not prioritize eating breakfast may have a different need for it. So that you can plan your day and begin it on a positive note, it is necessary that you develop habits that you find enjoyable and fulfilling. It would be futile for you to take on tasks that you will not enjoy, as this will not motivate you in any way, and on days when your subconscious attempts to convince you not to do something, you will give in because you are not enjoying the task. If you do not already have a firm plan for your morning routine, consider the following:

Meditating Eating a healthy breakfast Stretching Yoga Exercise, heavy or light Running Biking in a nearby park Reading Listening to audiobooks or music Learning something new Appreciate all that you have in the morning.

Specifically, there are numerous modes of meditation from which you can choose the one that suits you best. When you meditate, you allow yourself to gain greater insight, direction, and guidance on how and what to spend your time, which can exponentially improve your time management as you strive to become a better version of yourself. Therefore, by engaging in this practice first thing in the morning, you can actively plan and manage your time for productive purposes.

Chapter 10: Avoiding Delays Number

A tiny whiteboard hangs on the wall of my bedroom. A "today's" list, distinct from my overall "to do" list, comprises tasks that must be completed today. My "to do" list consists of fairly general tasks, such as having my car serviced and purchasing gifts for my loved ones. If "today" means immediately, I must get to work. It is acceptable to rearrange the timeline if doing so will improve efficiency. Having an exhaustive list of daily tasks keeps me on track to complete what must be done. My daily "today" section includes both meditation and physical activity. This appears to be beneficial.

Notes on Post-it notes. They can be used to monitor any number of tasks, either individually or in a list format (depending on the type of task at hand; I use both). When tasks must be completed sequentially, the stack can serve as a rudimentary ranking system. In fact, there is more: They can be easily rearranged, annotated, torn up, and re-posted on cork boards. They can be used as tokens, miniature whiteboards, or anything else that comes to mind. They can be transported easily and attached to other documents due to their small size. Additionally, having different colors for different types of tasks (as well as different annotations) is a wonderful visual aid. Lastly, they are inexpensive and, perhaps most importantly, simple (much simpler than software) to reconfigure as needs and initiatives change.

Never jeopardize everything on a single venture. Sometimes I ponder why individuals bring only one pen to $1,000-per-person conferences where they are paying to hear speakers. It's wonderful to have a backup plan in case something is lost, destroyed, or expires.

Utilize fewer assets.

Delegate. You must develop the ability to delegate significant responsibilities to others. Effective delegation will save you time and effort by making it simpler to monitor tasks that should have been delegated but weren't.

Now, your life depends on your decisions. Make the instruments and materials you employ serve you, as opposed to the other way around. Is it necessary for Outlook to scan for new messages every five minutes? Maybe, but I'm willing to bet that you'll accomplish much more if you verify it multiple times per day. The Blackberry is also included in this. Never neglect that you can find the ideal tool for your requirements; in fact, you can likely find multiple tools that would serve you well if you took the time to customize them.

Define roles and responsibilities with precision

This issue has plagued numerous initiatives, including my own, and I've finally realized why: Work is halted in the midst of the action due to a disagreement over who is responsible for what.

Perhaps a crucial user is delaying a crucial decision because she believes it is beyond her sphere of influence. Or, she may be hesitant to complete the task (such as delivering a presentation to the CEO) because she is not in her natural environment.

Finding the appropriate individual to perform the task or make the decision is essential in both instances. This is where your schedule begins to deviate because acquiring clarity can be time-consuming.

The following categories of concerns regarding accountability arise frequently:

There are two primary factors why someone may not want to do what is required: (1) They do not feel empowered to make a decision, or (2) They do not want to do the necessary task.

A person who lacks the necessary skills to perform a given job correctly.

The first stage is to define roles and expectations precisely. All team members should have a clear comprehension of their roles and responsibilities before beginning a project.

Include items such as communication ("I want you to regularly align with X", "I want you to host the X meeting", "I want you to meet with John from marketing once every two weeks"), and go over the responsibilities with each team member. This can be accomplished during a kickoff meeting, but an individual evaluation is preferable.

See also: Determining Project Roles and Responsibilities.

Maintain a detailed (and ruthless) record of the progress of your work.

Because I was always so persistent with follow-ups, people disliked me. I asked you every time we spoke, "Are you making progress with your data analysis?" Where can I locate the accepted standard?

I may not have made many friends by constantly nagging people to complete their assignments, but I believed it was the correct thing to do. It was ultimately my responsibility to ensure that the initiative would be launched on time. And the only method to ensure this would be to complete all tasks on time.

This method allows me to maintain track of the tasks I must complete for various projects.

Do you anticipate that your efforts will bear fruit? When monitoring production, you must be as meticulous and ruthless as feasible. Respecting your team members will motivate them to give their all. Be persistent and make it clear that this work must be accomplished by the agreed-upon deadline.

The advantage of maintaining a consistent routine of follow-up: You are aware of the current status of the assignment and possess the ability to resolve any issues that have arisen. When a colleague is experiencing difficulty, you can offer coaching, advice, or assistance. Regular follow-up can reduce or prevent delays.

Follow the instructions below:

Utilize a task management spreadsheet.

Establish a deadline and assign an individual to each duty. Multiple times per week, check in with the team (via email, phone, or in person). If something goes wrong with an undertaking, determine why it is not being completed. This could be due to a dearth of knowledge, a technical issue, the need for another person's input, or any number of other possibilities. Do what you can to resolve the issue.

Clarify mission requirements (and discuss transfer)

Tasks must be completed in a specific order when working on a project, with one task providing the output required by the next. The first order of business is to transport bricks and other construction materials. The next step is to construct the structure out of brickwork.

A time lag occurs when one process is unable to commence because its predecessor failed to produce the required results. In our case, the incorrect bricks were delivered, rendering house construction unfeasible.

In reality, specific conditions must be fulfilled in order for any given task to be accomplished successfully. If these conditions are not met, the previous step must be delayed until it has produced the required "output" before the subsequent step can commence.

My wife (a medical researcher) provided me with this second real-world example. In my wife's office, medical conditions are being analyzed statistically. Blood values are measured and utilized. Another team conducts the blood analysis, while my wife's team focuses on statistical analysis. The group analyzing the blood samples utilized the wrong chemical. Not compatible with the statistical methodologies utilized by my wife's organization. Due to this, months were squandered awaiting inaccurate whole blood analysis results (note: they are still waiting).

Steps to Follow: Ensure that each task's schedule specifies all necessary conditions and requirements. The worker will provide you with this information immediately ("I need X and

Y in order to complete the task"). Provide this information to the individual or individuals in command of the preceding activity. Better yet:

Gather the team members who have completed a series of tasks together. They must meet in person to discuss how they can collaborate most effectively and what each party requires from the other in terms of resources and ideas.

Participate in the most important project meetings

There are meetings that separate out from the routine project update meetings due to their importance. Unplanned meeting to discuss something that could spell the end of the endeavor. A meeting can be requested if a stakeholder is denied permission to endorse project work. These gatherings seem more like contests to me. If these meetings do not produce a solution, the endeavor may be terminated immediately.

These are meetings in which you must always participate as the project manager. If the matter is so crucial, you should organize the meeting. In this manner, you can regulate participation, exert your will over the conversation, and facilitate resolution.

Chapter 11: A Psychological Understanding Of Time Management

Your emotional foundation as a person Self-esteem is what is commonly referred to as how much you like yourself. How you perceive and feel about yourself has a significant impact on the quality of your existence. How you utilize your life and time to attain your fullest potential has a profound effect on your self-esteem. Your self-esteem rises when you are functioning effectively and falls when you are not. Self-efficacy is the opposite of self-esteem. It is the degree to which you believe you are competent, effective, and productive, able to solve your problems, carry out your work, and achieve your objectives. Along with these characteristics, your sense of competence, capability, and productivity will increase. The greater our sense of self, the more efficient and competent you will be according to Temporal Psychology, the more each one strengthens and supports the others. Those who successfully manage their time report feeling optimistic, assured, and in charge of their lives.

Principle of Management

The Law of Control is a simple principle that forms the basis of time management psychology. You should feel good about yourself to the extent that you believe you have control over your existence, according to this law. This law also states that you have less self-assurance if you believe you have no control over your life or career.

Psychologists differentiate between an internal locus of control, in which you feel in command of your own destinies, and an external locus of control, in which you feel subject to external forces. You have an external locus of control if you believe that your boss, your expenses, the stress of your job, and your responsibilities control you. You believe you do not have true control over your time or your life, and that you have too much to do in too little time. The majority of your daily activities consist of reacting and responding to external occurrences. Self-determined and goal-directed action differs significantly from reaction, which is an immediate response to external stimuli. It is the difference between feeling upbeat and in control of your life and feeling down, stressed, and under strain. To perform at your highest level, you must have complete control over both your professional and personal affairs.

Your Emotions and Ideas

According to psychological theory, every person has a self-concept, or internal master program, that governs their behavior in all significant spheres. High self-concept time managers perceive and believe that they are productive and well-organized individuals. They have considerable influence over their daily activities and employment.

Your self-concept consists of all of your thoughts, perceptions, and beliefs about who you are, especially in relation to your time management skills. Some individuals believe they are extremely organized and productive. Others are perpetually overburdened by the expectations of others and their surroundings.

Beliefs Drive Reality

How do you feel about yourself and your time management skills? Do you believe that you are a highly competent and effective time manager? Do you believe that your productivity is high and that you have complete command over your life and work? Regardless of your perspective, if you believe you are an excellent time manager, your actions will naturally reflect this belief. A healthy self-concept is necessary if you wish to attain congruence between your inner and outer selves. If you believe you effectively manage your time, you will be an excellent time manager. No matter how many time management courses you take, books you read, or strategies you implement, nothing will help if you believe you are a poor time manager. If you have a pattern of being late for meetings and engagements, or if you believe you are disorganized, these behaviors will become routine. If you do not alter your perceptions of your personal levels of effectiveness and efficiency, your ability to manage your time will not change.

Make a decision

How do you generate new, optimistic beliefs about your identity and productivity? Thankfully, it is not difficult. Simply employ desire, decisiveness, determination, and discipline. Decide to develop a particular time management habit, such as consistently arriving early to meetings. Every change you experience in your life is the result of a deliberate decision to act differently. The first significant stage is deciding to learn effective time management techniques.

Develop your intellect

Once you have decided to become a highly productive individual, you can implement a variety of personal programming techniques. Start by modifying your internal dialogue. Your thoughts about yourself determine 95% of your emotions and consequent actions the majority of the time. Take a break whenever you feel overworked and convince yourself, "I am extremely organized and productive." If asked how you invest your time, you should respond, "I am an exceptional time manager." time and time again. Every time you declare, "I am well organized," your subconscious interprets this as a command and begins encouraging and pushing you to adopt well-organized behaviors.

Chapter 12: Time Management For Enhanced Productivity

Do not forget that, despite the fact that we have limited resources, the possibilities are limitless. We are competent of a vast array of productive activities. To eliminate some unimportant items, we must make swift decisions. When we feel superhumanly occupied, we acknowledge this fact. However, we are limited in our capabilities. The debris requires cleaning.

Everything that hinders our ability to live is disorder. We cannot perform the most essential tasks as a result. We are occupied by trivial matters, but they do not help us achieve our objectives. Additionally, clutter must be addressed. The most significant factors will influence your decisions and time allocation. Why persist with a path if you are unaware of your destination? Before developing your strategy, you must determine your goals and the rules you will follow.

After determining your objective, you may contemplate your route to that objective. The selection of your goals is crucial. However, if you do not go the extra mile and create a plan for achieving your objectives, they will never become a reality.

2.1 The Focus Method

We can only accomplish so much. Despite our limited resources, the possibilities are vast. To eliminate specific items, we must make crucial decisions. While we feel inhumanly busy, we acknowledge this as a fact. However, our capabilities are constrained. The debris requires cleaning.

Clutter is anything that prevents us from living the lives we desire. We can no longer continue. The trivial activities occupy our time but do not advance our objectives. It must also be removed.

After determining your objective, you may contemplate your route to that objective. The selection of your goals is crucial. However, if you do not go the extra mile and create a plan to attain your objectives, they will remain as dreams.

Plan your route to your destination. To accomplish your objectives, you must select the optimal strategy. You must select the necessary activities and resources. We risk succumbing to our environment and coasting through existence if we do not.

Knowing the correct action is not sufficient. Additionally, you must be aware of prohibited conduct. We've already determined that time is of the essence. We must determine how we will utilize all of our time. In order to say "yes" to other things, we must say "no" to some. There will inevitably be circumstances that cause us to deviate from our goals and abandon them. Sometimes, these obstacles may result from unhealthy behaviors. Sometimes they are created by those who wish for the failure of everyone. They could also be triggered by less-than-ideal positive characteristics. Regardless of the source of the obstacles, we must thoroughly evaluate each one and determine which actions must be halted. Examine yourself to determine what makes you special. What brings you to life? What gives you a sense of existence and convinces you that users are more than just check-writing robots? What makes your emotions hurt? It may be writing, singing, dancing, drawing, jogging, weightlifting, or something else that inspires you to express your highest priorities.

The Focus Formula

One thing you cannot return to the past. In the Bible, "redeeming the time" refers to making the most of time. We do not know how long we have been in this country. Consequently, we must maximize it. Due to the constant barrage of interruptions, genuine requirements, and diversions, we must dedicate ourselves to enhancing our organizational skills.

We have several uncompleted tasks on our to-do lists, but it is too simple to waste time. Too often, we become engulfed in a maelstrom of activity, only to discover at the end of the day that we have not accomplished what we intended. Our strongest inclination is to put off completing the most challenging but necessary task. In other words, it may not be simple to consistently manage the numerous responsibilities, activities, and people we encounter on a daily basis while also completing the most important tasks.

The majority of books on time management aim to teach you how to arrange and organize your tasks so that you can complete everything on your to-do list. This strategy is impracticable. If you attempt to accomplish everything, you run the risk of burning out and becoming ineffective!

The first step is acknowledging that you cannot do everything. This implies that you will complete fewer tasks, decline requests, decline certain initiatives, and reduce your to-do list. If you want to complete the most essential tasks, you must set goals and devote the majority of your focus and energy to attaining them.

Examining what you are currently focusing on and what you have been wasting time on is the first step in completing the appropriate duties. This requires a careful examination of your actual decision and a clear understanding of your top priorities. Since it will serve as the foundation for your daily, quarterly, and annual goals and plans, you should devote a great deal of time and effort to developing it.

In general, you should determine your primary objectives for the year, also known as your concentration regions. There are likely categories for effort and categories for personal affairs. Avoid selecting too many areas of concentration because you cannot manage them all. When organizing your daily, monthly, and recurring duties, it is helpful to allocate the majority of your efforts to specific focus areas. This will ensure that your daily actions align with your professional and personal long-term objectives.

To become a maestro of time management, you must understand your obstacles. Every day, we face multiple interruptions, not to mention the variety of time management issues and diversions that technology has made available to us. What type of squanderer are you? Is Facebook to blame for this? TV? YouTube? What time of day do you typically utilize social media? What about computer games? Perhaps culinary shows? Keeping abreast of sporting events and outcomes? Internet browsing at random? Are you interested in prominent news? The list could be endless. All of the aforementioned can squander countless hours of your valuable time. Several specialists recommend considering the amount of time spent on these activities in a particular week to determine where it went. If you want to improve your time management skills, you must monitor how much money you spend on time-consuming and potentially addictive activities. Then, devise a plan to reduce or restrict your usage, such as turning off your devices at certain times to maximize your concentration.

It's not as if these pastimes or technologies are evil or inappropriate; many of them serve a purpose or are enjoyable pastimes. You should determine how much of your schedule you wish to devote to these activities, but you also need time to relax. This is a productive use of your time. These activities will unquestionably need to be scaled back or abandoned if you are determined to achieve your objective. Recognize the time you expend on these activities and how it prevents you from achieving your goals.

Many of us suffer from this because we desire to assist our coworkers and friends with their requirements. There are requests from every direction, and we wish to assist. It is challenging to deny. Despite our best efforts, there are only 24 hours in a day, so we will not be able to complete everything on our to-do lists before going to bed.

God gives us a limited amount of time each day, and regardless of how much you should be doing or how much you want to aid others, you can only accomplish so much. Avoid overcommitting yourself and placing yourself at risk. This causes you to feel overwhelmed, anxious, and unable to produce quality work. According to research, individuals are more likely to complete a task if they are informed beforehand of its difficulty, complexity, and duration.

Make a concerted effort to be truthful about the time it will take you to complete a project if you accept another assignment and whether you will meet the deadline. With a well-maintained to-do list, you can keep track of your obligations. Finally, it would be ideal if you could say "no" when required. By declining potentially overwhelming tasks, your long-term capacity to complete significant, high-quality work, maintain focus, and be sufficiently rested to engage in discussions, creative problem-solving, and other activities will be preserved.

Regardless of how well you believe you manage your time, you can always do better. Some of us have been working six days per week and are content. However, this does not inherently imply that we were productive. Making the most of your time does not necessitate studying continuously for hours or performing multiple tasks simultaneously. Working intelligently (rather than harder) and improving your natural attention can allow you to accomplish much more, complete tasks with a higher level of quality, and gain more time.

Chapter 13: Combine Tasks

The majority of people have learned to multitask in order to remain competitive and relevant in the modern world. This can help you accomplish many tasks in a short period of time if done correctly. Despite the difficulty, combining tasks can enhance an individual's focus, skills, and ability to execute tasks accurately.

Blend it
If you have a list of tasks to complete, the most efficient way to accomplish them is to couple the tasks that are most closely related and require similar execution methods. As a result, the individual will be able to concentrate on a specific interconnected area before proceeding to the next phase of the task framework.
Correctly combining duties can also reduce the amount of time required to complete the "list" of chores.
It should be noted, however, that the framework included in each assignment

must be as closely related as possible; otherwise, they run the risk of completely mucking up the entire undertaking, necessitating a redo. Obviously, this is a disastrous outcome that must be prevented at all costs. As a consequence, a certain amount of discernment is required when outlining the potential pairings of the activities.

Most women, particularly mothers, can attest to the daily necessity of managing multiple responsibilities. Unsurprisingly, the majority of mothers have become adept at combining and accomplishing tasks efficiently and quickly.

The majority of men and women are proficient at juggling multiple responsibilities in the workplace. In the majority of contexts and situations, it is nearly obligatory to accomplish as much as feasible in the shortest amount of time.

Chapter 5: Top Time Management Strategies

Determine a course of action by identifying your most time-consuming duties and analyzing whether or not you are focusing on the most important tasks. Realistically preparing for and estimating the time allotted for other tasks may be made easier if you are aware of how much effort is expended on typical tasks.

Creating a "to-do" list is a straightforward way to prioritize your duties. Your lifestyle will determine if you require a daily, monthly, or annual list. Ensure that your chart does not become unmanageable. Instead of making a list of objectives or multi-step strategies, create a list of manageable sections. You can classify objects as being of high, medium, or low priority, number items in order of significance, or use a color-coding system.

Experts in time management recommend using a personal planning instrument to boost your productivity. Personal forecasting techniques include organizers, diaries, mobile applications, charts, notecards, portable diaries, and journals. By writing down your activities, plans, and items to memorize, you can free up your mind to concentrate on your goals. Listeners may choose to express their views in lieu of speaking. The key is to select a single organized, practical solution and adhere to it.

Inefficiency in time management is the consequence of disorganization. Studies have shown that clutter has a negative effect on an individual's sense of well-being. Organize yourself to improve your time management.

5.1 The Eisenhower Box

Being occupied does not imply that one is productive. You may spend many hours extinguishing fires, but remain uncommitted to attaining your long-term goals. This activity is time-consuming and emotionally draining. The issue is a failure to establish priorities. Regardless of the long-term benefits, humans prioritize time-sensitive tasks above all others.

The Eisenhower Structure is a fundamental decision-making tool that will assist you in distinguishing between duties that are essential, not essential, urgent, and non-urgent. It separates tasks into four categories, indicating which should be prioritized first and which will be delegated or eliminated.

Stephen Covey popularized it in his book The Seven Habits of Highly Successful People, also known as the Urgent-Important Matrix. It was named after America's 34th president, Dwight Eisenhower, who was known for his efficiency and organization. Eisenhower Dwight is rumored to have prioritized his responsibilities, as only the most vital and urgent matters reached his desk.

The Eisenhower Matrix employs this same concept to distinguish between the essential and urgent tasks on your to-do list, which you can then delegate or ignore.

The basis of the matrix is the distinction between urgent and important duties.

Urgent tasks require your urgent attention and are time-sensitive. It is an inventory of tasks that you feel obligated to perform. When you focus on important tasks, you become sensitive, which can make you feel protective, rushed, and constrained.

Important tasks result in the long-term missions, beliefs, and objectives of your organization. It is possible that they will not yield immediate results. Important matters are occasionally, but not always, time-sensitive. By placing you in a receptive state of mind, focusing on essential tasks can help you feel calm, reasonable, and receptive to new ideas.

People have a tendency to believe that all essential tasks are equally important, but this is not always the case. This misconception may be the result of our propensity to focus on imminent problems and obstacles.

Four of Eisenhower's Quadrants Matrix

The Initial quadrant

The first quadrant is the "do" quadrant, which is where you will place all essential and significant tasks. Place in this box any task on your to-do list that must be completed immediately, has evident consequences, and impacts your long-term objectives.

There must be no ambiguity regarding which jobs pertain to this industry, as these are the ones on your mind and presumably causing you the most anxiety.

Arrangement - The Second Quadrant

The second quadrant is the "schedule" square, where you will list all non-urgent but essential tasks. Some tasks can be deferred because they have an impact on your long-term objectives but do not need to be completed immediately.

These tasks will be performed after the tasks in quadrant one have been completed. To complete the assignment in this subject area, you can utilize a variety of time management techniques.

Representative – The Third Quadrant

Quadrant 3 is the "delegate" quadrant. Here, you will place any imperative but unimportant tasks. These tasks must be completed immediately, but they have little bearing on your long-term objectives.

You may delegate these tasks to other team members because you lack a close relationship with them and they are unlikely to accept your specialized skill set. Delegating tasks is one of the most efficient ways to reduce your workload while allowing your team to acquire new skills.

Delete - Quadrant Four

After reviewing your to-do list and assigning tasks to the first three regions, you will have a few remaining tasks. The positions that have been eliminated were not necessary.

These trivial, non-urgent diversions only hinder your ability to accomplish your goals. Place the remaining items on your to-do lists in the "delete" quadrant of your to-do lists.

Let's suppose Julie is the chief program manager for a corporation of average size. She manages a large team, interacts with customers, submits reports to her superiors, is married, and has two children, all while attempting to consume and live healthily. It is reasonable to assume that Julie will not be able to achieve all of her objectives. However, she can use the matrix to determine her goals and how to cope with changes to her plans.

Consider the Eisenhower Matrix at Work.

Julie organized her views using the time-management skills matrix as follows:

She was unable to check her email in the early morning because the stand-up session revealed QA divisional issues. She categorized the messages rather than marking them as something to discuss later because discussing a strategy was more crucial.

The customer who was scheduled to meet with Julie at noon arrived half an hour late to ask specific questions. She was aware that her son's field trip was still several weeks away, so she did not require information immediately. She could possibly discuss it with the instructor later that day. She rescheduled the appointment for 11:30 a.m. and the phone call for later so as not to keep her client waiting.

It became apparent around 4:00 p.m. that certain aspects of the undertaking required immediate attention. In contrast, Julie's son had fallen ill again the week prior and required medical attention. She delegated the responsibility of organizing the conference to her most reliable colleague because her son's health took precedence.

Consider the Eisenhower Matrix at Home.

Despite having an appointment, Tom and Julie had to wait longer for their test because the doctor's office was full. Julie asked her husband to do the grocery purchasing in case they were unable to complete it on time; Julie wanted to improve her overall fitness, so she worked out three times per week. However, as she was departing the office, a coworker called to remind her of their previous conversation. Some of their decisions required authorization. Julie rescheduled her workout so she could participate in a video conference with a few of the late-night workers.

Today, assisting them in finishing so they could return home was more important and imperative than her exercise.

By 9:30 p.m., Julie was exhausted from visitors, conferences, the health clinic, and her children's activities. She desired nothing more than a restful night's slumber. She decided not to watch the movie because she knew that sleeping would benefit her far more than viewing television at that time.

As illustrated by Julie's diagram, the purpose of the time matrix is to teach us all how to make better decisions regarding our schedules. She did not need to overthink the tasks or the consequences of her actions because she knew precisely what she was doing. She was able to effectuate necessary alterations in a seamless and stress-free manner.

What Sets the Time Matrix Apart from Other Methods?

This strategy has nothing to do with acquiring new skills and everything to do with enhancing your reasoning. It will assist you in gaining a clearer understanding of your goals and how you spent your time or contributed to your current position. Thus, you will be better able to coordinate and plan for the future.

It will result in a positive change after some time has elapsed. You will observe how much easier it is to plan your work and how much more adept you have become at handling minor setbacks and impending constraints.

Attempting to manage time is becoming obsolete in some respects. Coaches and efficiency experts recommend that you have the ability to manage your objectives and resources. We cannot create time because we lack it. Simply stated, we can utilize it more effectively. Instead of cramming as much as possible into a day, prioritize the essentials.

5.2 Warren Buffett's "2 List" Strategy

It can be exciting and motivating to write down your life objectives. It provides us with direction, clarifies our objectives, makes us all feel active, and gives the impression that we are advancing.

Have you ever created an inventory of your goals only to find that it was lengthy? Then, once action is taken, they are either forgotten or only partially accomplished? We are taught from a tender age to set goals; however, do all of these objectives limit us?

Buffet, one of the world's finest businessmen, questions the necessity of these goals. Rather, he attributes his success to eliminating irrelevant goals in order to focus on those that will lead to the desired outcomes.

With a net worth of more than seventy billion dollars and ownership of more than seventy businesses through his private equity firm Berkshire Hathaway, Warren Buffett has demonstrated that he knows a thing or two about prioritizing essential work.

This level of concentration does not, however, occur frequently. When there are numerous options available, the majority of us experience choice anxiety. Buffett has a solution, however.

According to a story told by Buffett's private pilot, Mike Flint, Buffett has a straightforward method for determining which work merits his attention. While Flint inquired as to which professional objectives should be prioritized, this strategy was implemented for both short- and long-term objectives.

When Flint and Buffett were discussing this endeavor, he consented to prioritize the five objectives Buffett had highlighted. However, because the remaining 20 were still important to him, he stated that he would work on them whenever he had the chance.

That is comprehensible. They were not terrible choices, but they were not among the top five. What was Buffett's refutation?

"No, Mike, you have it inverted. The items you did not circle comprised your list of items to avoid. You will not give attention to this information until you have completed your top five."

www.ingramcontent.com/pod-product-compliance
Lightning Source LLC
Chambersburg PA
CBHW050243120526
44590CB00016B/2200